Passion of Poetry

Beloved Isles

By Maureen Brindle

*"Love the essence of our being,
Dreams are what we're seeing."*

www.maureenbrindlepoetry.com

Beloved Isles
Copyright © Maureen Brindle 2013

All rights reserved

No part of this book may be reproduced in any form by photocopying or any electronic or mechanical means, including information storage or retrieval systems, without permission in writing from the copyright owner.

ISBN-13:978-1492951087

ISBN-10:1492951080

First Published 2013

Printed by Create Space,

An Amazon.com Company

Passion of poetry flowing free,

Like life in the Eternal sea.

By
Maureen Brindle

Acknowledgements
Beloved Isles
Thanks to my husband and family for all their support.
Jeannette Slavinski U.K. Humanitarian Ambassador for W.C.H. U.S.A & founder. www.thenakedgoddess.com
Read my poetry in The Naked Goddess Anthology in support of Help for Heroes U.K. & Wounded Warriors Project U.S.A . Available worldwide. Thanks to Lt Norman Harris.
Grateful thanks to U.S. poet, illustrator & novelist Patricia Eichler; Illustrator of my children's narrative poetry book Missy Cat's Christmas Fairy, available worldwide www.amazon.com
Prize winning poet Rachel Davies & East Manchester and Tameside Stanza of The Poetry Society have been my steady support & www.thepoetrysociety.com London.
Also thanks to David Peek, Rokib Uddin and the presenters at Tameside Radio for your help recording & broadcasting my poetry. Chrisoula Sirigou, European Lunch, Redshift Radio for having me read at her events and on her international radio show.
.Thanks to H.H. Princess Maria Amor, founder of the worldwide charity, We Care for Humanity U. S. A. & Global Officials of Dignity Awards, Los Angeles Head Representative of the World Peace Committee California & Doctor Dawn Gibbins M.B.E appointed Pioneer to the Life of our Nation by her Majesty Queen Elizabeth. Thanks to Antonio Franchitti for his support.
Thanks to all my friends all over the world. I wish I could name you all.
Best wishes
Maureen Brindle
www.maureenbrindlepoetry.com

Contents

Acknowledgements 8

Contents 9

Welcome to Beloved Isles 15

World War, a Hundred Years 16

Beloved Isles 18

Coronation of Queen Elizabeth 20

Memories 22

Faith 24

Prince Phillip 25

The Queen Mum 26

William Shakespeare 27

Robert Burns 28

Jubilee Pageant 30

Comet 32

Evening Alphabet 33

Dance 34

Spring Temptations 35

Summer 36

Autumn Fall 37

Winter 38

Ode to the Moon 39

Sun Dance 40

Dove Stones Reservoir 41

Morcambe Bay 42

Rings in the Rain 43

Olympic Games, London 2012 44

Freedom 45

Greece 46

Paris France 48

Marbella Spain 49

Spanish Dance 50

Rio de Janeiro 52

Saint Patrick's Day 53

Peridot 54

Holiday Romance 55

Beautiful World 56

Bluebell Days 57

Along the River 58

A Lonely Beach 59

Stale Bread 60

Holocaust 61

W. W.2 True Account 62

Amour 63

Dawn above the Cheshire Plain 64

So Precious Our Love 66

Pre-Historic Storm 67

Titanic, a Hundred Years 68

Angel Light 70

Diana, Queen of Hearts 71

Prince George, Born to be King 72

Baptism Day 73

Saint Clement Danes, London. 74

Memorial to Bomber Command 75

Accession Day Diamond Jubilee [6/2/2012] 76

Angel Stone 77

The Goddess of the Sand 78

Cry for Freedom 79

Poppy 80

Mam 82

The Rose 83

Welcome to this World 84

Steam Train 85

City of Manchester 86

Smudge 87

Charlie Chuck, Bombing Raid. 88

The Faces of War 90

Van Barfoot Hero [1919-2012] 91

Afghanistan War 92

America 93

President Obama 94

Abraham Lincoln 95

President John F. Kennedy 96

Remember the Souls of 9/11 98

Remember Vietnam 99

Curiosity Rover 100

The American Princess 101

Dark Matter 102

Perfect Storm 103

Moon Landing 104

Pope Francis 106

Aberfan 1966-2012 107

Nelson Mandela 108

Bonfire Night 109

Silver Rains 110

Ouija Board 111

Clock Tower 112

The Cutty Sark 113

Emblem 114

Cat Woman 115

House Viewing 116

The Loving Cup 117

Sergeant Major Jack 118

Solomon Browne Penlee [19/12/1981] 120

Lilac Days 121

Tsunami 122

Vesuvius Eruption 123

The Unknown Soldier 124

Fallen Heroes 125

Sir Winston Churchill 126

Hell for Men 127

The Falkland's War 1982 128

Syria 129

Slavery 130

Holy Rain 131

Only a Winters Tale 132

Presents 133

Christmas Night 134

Christmas Joy 135

The Ghost of Christmas Past 136

The Spirit of Christmas Present 137

Christmas Future 138
Pirate Ship 140
Passion Flower 141
The Spirit of Love 142
The Ghostly Coal Miner 143
Love and War 144
Night Witch 145
Honey 146
Dreams 147
St. Joan of Arc [1412-1431] 148
Thank you 151

Welcome to Beloved Isles

Passion of poetry all around,
Ethereal, emotional, soothing sound,
Any subject under the sun,
Deep dreams of love and fun.

Passion fashions its enduring dance,
Fantasy, stories enhance.
A rose for the People's Princess,
A poem for London Olympic success.

True heroes stand tall,
Written on the eternal wall.
Ghost stories, just for fun,
Praise for love under the sun.

Celebrating Queen Elizabeth's Diamond Jubilee.
Celebrating the beautiful world we see.
President Kennedy, heroes of war,
Social sadness and more.

Dreams through the seasons,
Bravery without reasons,
Loves heated dance,
Wonder, romance.

Every emotion you can feel,
Poetic dreams make it real.
Is it heaven or is it hell,
The skeleton ringing the eternal bell?

I hope you enjoy "Beloved Isles."
Maureen Brindle.

World War, a Hundred Years

Deep down the soldiers sleep,
The flower of youth in Ypres.
The graveyards of Belgium and France,
Flanders' poppy fields, sunlight dance.

Serving soldiers lined in rows,
Scarlet sunset's golden glows.
Eternal soldiers they became,
First World War battle flame.

From around the world they came,
Soldiers of freedom they became.
A hundred years now they lie,
Hearing the eternal battle cry.

War to end all wars, it became,
Your country needs you, just the same.
My great grandfather & granddad returned.
Many brave comrades were interred.

Sixteen million born to die,
New weaponry, no food supply.
Fighting for freedom, beloved land,
Blessed by God's Holy Hand.

Marne began. trench warfare's birth,
Fighting for every inch of earth.
In machine guns' muddy hell,
The heroes fought and fell.
The Somme, Passchendaele, Verdun, Gallipoli gave,
Battlefields' unknown soldiers' unmarked graves.
Youth is the poppy precious gem,
Forever we will remember them.

Passion of Poetry

Beloved Isles

Land of spiritual fire,
Symbolic rose of desire,
Meandering meadows, beautiful braid,
Green grass and wheat fields fade.

Blessed by rushing rivers,
Sunlight's shining slithers,
Cumulous clouds, a breathless bed,
God above our halcyon head.

Coltsfoot's wild yearning yellow,
Daffodil's ringing bellow,
Skips into summer's gaudy glow,
Gardens glorious, lawns to mow.

September's colours paint these isles,
With yellow and orange smiles.
Rustling autumn's foot falls,
As bare armed winter calls.

The streets, empty moonlight shed,
Predatory footfalls ahead
For those without a blossomed bed,
Ice cold snow and tears to shed.

Fear frenzied wandering way,
Hope harried, dismal day,
Streets paved with gold,
The story so often told.

The Shard's shine pierces the sky,
The revolving London Eye,
The River Thames rhythmic flow,
Reflects starlight's stolid glow.

She breathes her beauty from candle-shine,
Across the centuries soaked with wine.
Parchment words formed the base,
Of our lovely Land's loyal grace.

Castles and palaces stand,
Great Cathedrals bless our land,
Whilst the flourishing future lies,
In a new born baby's eyes.

Diamond Jubilee

Coronation of Queen Elizabeth

Sixty years from the Coronation,
Queen Elizabeth, Jewel of our Nation,
Elizabethan era of colossal creation,
Worldwide, wondrous celebration.

Queen of our Commonwealth,
Inspiration of spiritual wealth.
Sixty years for the world to share,
Stoic service without compare.

Ruling a Diamond Elizabethan age,
Technology turning the plastic page.
Changing Land, Sea and Sky,
Changing as the years go by.

1953, a beautiful queen for all to see,
Swore an oath of patriotic loyalty.
Crowned in magnificent majesty,
Ordained by God's Holy ministry.

Westminster Abbey's historical setting,
For the Queen's Coronation blessing,
The Coronation Stone in place,
Historical unity of our race.

Bejewelled beauty, holy blest,
Loyalty our Queen invests.
For her people our Queen reigns,
Shining diamond amongst sovereigns.

Frankel, Ascot's jubilee star,
Enhanced the year, raised the bar.
Continuing our Jubilee celebrations,
Joyous jubilee recreations.

We swear our loyalty to the Queen,
Our representative serenely seen.
History's finest monarch blest.
Simply put she is the best.

Memories

Snowdon rises from the sea,
Majestic eagles flying free,
Beauty in the bubbling stream,
Shady pools, dulcet dreams.

Fish bubbles, circling world,
Rippling rivers, flowers unfurled.
The smell of summer in the air,
Fairy castles, hermit's prayer.

Baby lambs on the beach,
Gambling just out of reach.
Gorgeous green up to the sky,
Where the swooping gulls cry.

Conway castle, historic hill,
Skylark rising's soulful trill.
Caught on the thermal air.
Rising to the plateau there.

Down to the stony quayside,
Fishing boats, side by side.
Folding, mending nets,
Serene scene, time forgets.

The Pilot from Liverpool Bay,
Escorts a liner the safest way,
The train line hugs the coast,
Magnificent scenery it boasts.

Dolphins jump in the salty air,
Music in the mountains fair,
Welsh dragons, mystery, might,
St. David's land, holy light.

Deep, coal darkness, souls to heaven,
Abervan's village heart is broken.
Coal's deadly, slagheap slide,
Children with the Lord abide.

Deep beneath the earth they toil,
Where coal, gas and air embroil,
Cramped, wet and cracking coal,
Miners pay the heavy toll.

The valleys' song in the heart,
In bravery, they stand apart.
Great land of mountainous beauty,
Princedom, Guards, civic duty.

Carnarvon Castle, painted by the sun,
Where the years of history begun.
Coastline of a mermaid's dream,
Verdant islands, silver stream.

Cardiff capital, historic dock,
City where the people flock
Cardiff Barrage waves its way,
Salmon return through Cardiff bay.

Welsh dragons, mystery, might,
St. David's land, beaming bright.

Faith

Faith is a liquid living fire,
Light of the world to inspire.
Illuminates the darkest night,
Drives the fight for right.

Faith is the gold in the ring,
The hope that love brings,
Drive implementing dreams,
Bedrock of grace streams.

Faith transcends life's call,
To live for, Faith is over all.
Belief is our people's purpose bright,
God, country, ideals, fight for right.

So in the shining, sunlight stream,
The golden shadows of the dream,
They bond the faith to the earth.
The hallowed purpose of our birth.

Prince Phillip

We all loudly cheer,
Prince Phillip we hold dear.
He tell it how he sees it.
He doesn't hide or breeze it.

Newspapers die of shock,
The people think he rocks.
Those who dare not laugh,
Can look at their circulation graph!

People see a Prince of Men,
Dependable, not in a pen.
Dutiful prince of our land,
Prince in popular demand.

His mother, a graceful princess,
In a nun's plain dark dress,
An example to us all,
In serving others we walk tall.

The gracious gift is love,
Mirroring God above,
From our hearts freely given,
Pure as the snow is driven.

The Queen Mum

For over a century she graced our lands,
Empress, Queen Consort, commands,
With love, elegance and flair,
For the country's needs without compare.

Bowes Lyon beauty, sunlight rays,
She was beloved all her days,
Affectionately called the Queen Mum,
Mother of the Nation by some.

Young, she lost her beloved King,
Married to the Monarchy, stability to bring.
Through the Second World War, she bravely stayed,
In London, the people homage paid.

She loved betting and horse racing.
She understood what the people were facing.
Her sunny smile crossed the Ocean,
Elizabeth, Queen Mum, devout devotion.

William Shakespeare

William Shakespeare, poet of past time,
So many plays, rhyme most sublime,
Stories readily replay,
In life and fiction every day.

Your wise words slip from the tongue,
Your definitions of right and wrong,
Give and take, no mistake,
Mercy for Justice's sake.

West Side story, your glory,
The Romeo and Juliet story.
Star crossed lovers still exist,
Lovers lost and not kissed.

Tempest, Midsummer Night's Dream,
Your fairy wisdoms with reality gleam.
How many Titanias truly make,
The same blind love mistake?

Shining, sultry shards of sunny light,
Trickle in a world of hum-drum trite,
Our Great Bard, identity maligned,
A rose by any other name we find.

The globe theatre still magic today,
Voile veils of vanishing affray,
The spirit of the historic play.
Reminders of St. Crispin's Day.

Before Agincourt you must recall,
Valued valiance voiced for all.

Robert Burns

Sometimes I feel you in my head,
My heart knows you're long dead.
I see how my Granddad signed his name,
Your signature was just the same.

I am your shadows footfall,
I hear the rolling years call.
To you I owe my poetic art,
The shade of your big heart.

When you whisper in my ear,
I pretend not to hear.
With words I nearly drown,
Until I write them down.

Can I put the blame on you?
When poetic dreams, don't come true?
Every New Year your song resounds,
Auld Lang Syne your joke abounds.

When they pipe the Haggis be proud,
Hardship, condemnation condensed in a cloud.
For your love, we love thee,
Scotland, Burns Night, Haggis, thee.

The Ritz Burns Night Celebration,
Gifted tickets, deliberation.
I met my one true love.
You smiling from above.

Maybe because I was the first to be,
Without the Burns name, you see.
You whisper to me the art.
You, forever in my heart.

Passion of Poetry

Jubilee Pageant

Jubilee pageant, Thames River flows,

The steel sky above rain bestows.

Triumphant trumpets fill the air,

HMS Belfast moored there.

14,000 tons on Russian Convoys,

Lifted by the great ocean buoy.

Propellers whirling in the air,

Memories lie vivid there.

The Avenue of Sail, the Tall Ships,

Wait mast muster, bunting dips,

Venetian Gondoliers, historic crafts,

Tug boats, before and aft.

The Spirit of Chartwell, the Queens Royal Barge

Flowers fill, red and gold montage,

Follows the row boats, the Gloriana is seen.

HMS President awaits the Queen.

Rain sheets on the river fleets
Jubilee spirit again repeats.
Thames clipper boats, narrow boats,
1000 crafts, everything that floats.

Even Dunkirk little rescue ships.
As the music barge smoothly slips,
Under Tower Bridge proclaim,
The vocal voice of shipping fame.

Echoing horns midst the misty air,
Seafaring sounds aloft aware.
Shard slipping into misty mirage skies,
The red ensign fluttering flies.

A Sword Fish Bi-plane and helicopter display,
Cancelled as it's such a dismal day.
Historic London cheers the way,
Great pageant, Queen's Diamond Jubilee Day

Comet

Dipping dynamite projects,
Searing stalagmite reflects,
The rushing city race,
The pushing pretty face.

Dreams dangling, arid air,
Teams tangling, solid stare,
Every night they push,
In the rising red rush.

Holding the hurried height,
Folding the flurried flight,
The mystery in the snow flakes,
The shivery frozen lakes.

Spilled by moonbeams,
Entrapped in dreams,
The comets fiery tail,
In the night sky's starry trail.

Emblazoned in the fire, light dance,
A million years of night romance.
Lover's wishing on a shooting star,
Light dust display tortuous far.

In the universe's awesome scale
Lovers' trysts projections pale.
Prismatic projection skimmed the sky,
Clarion Comet, hydrodynamic high.

Evening Alphabet

Along the riverbank they drink,
Beyond blended sunsets sink,
Crying gulls swoop across the sea,
Dizzily dipping, flying free.
Elevation in the hot night air,
Frustration's fancy there,
Gracefully glancing everywhere,
Helium heights without a care.
Indigo skies, dapper days,
Jealously jostling moonlight haze,
Kismet kisses, star blessed mirth,
Long shadows shade the earth.
Meanings derived by man,
Notions of nations' perennial plan.
Omnipotent in loving arms,
Planet Earth's worldly charms.
Quaking reeling power,
Rotating earthy hour,
Sun pulls the earth's wandering way,
Trailing comets starlit stay.
Under a shallow scalloped edge,
Voluptuous earth's promise pledge.
Winged angels the promise prize,
Xenophobic countries arise.
Young couples speak of love,
Zenith zircon shines above.

.

Dance

Let's Dance on the hot sand,
Let's dance on the grass land.
Bare feet, eyes meet,
Twist and shake and greet.
Swing around the hearty oak,
Where angels spoke.
Under the sun and stars we dance,
In the heat, in a trance.
Come and take a chance,
Love, dream and dance.
Feel your happy heartbeat,
To the rhythm of your feet.
Dance the days of lovely light.
Dance the days of blossom bright.
Dance all the snow away,
Dance along the tidal spray.
The world turns to the beat,
The beat of dancing feet.
Dance the clouds in the sky,
Dance the fields of wheat and rye.
Spin the clouds of dancing day,
Dance all the blues away,
Dance the live long day.
Dance under the magic moon,
Dance together in tune,
Dance until the angels swoon.
Dance to love's tactile tune.
Dance in the ice and fire,
Dance to the music of the lyre.

Spring Temptations

Temptations Goddess spring intense,
Bewitching every sultry sense.
Bestowing love in the bower,
Pollinating every fluffy flower.

Naked dreams winter stripped,
Spring temptress nectar sipped.
Love sparkles in the balmy breeze,
Loves magic in the eddy ease.

Rippling like a moonlight melody,
Softly sailing on the sunny sea.
Temptations Goddess raises her head,
From the Earth's birth bower bed.

Heady perfume, Muses mist,
What mortal could resist?
Hypnotic dreams, soulful eyes,
Budding beauty from the skies.

Temptress beauty, lazy lay,
Basking brightness of the day,
Feeling the movement of the earth,
Tempting Goddess, mystic mirth.

Summer

Summer's hazy goddess smiles,
Dappled blue, the earth beguiles.
She casts her gown of light,
In the hot and steamy night.

Garlands of golden roses grace,
Her shining sun kissed lace.
Flowers grow beneath her feet,
Butterflies bask in the heat.

Fluttering from flower to flower,
The wonderment of the bower.
Birds rising in the thermal air,
Floating on cushions without a care.

The lazy, love-kissed days,
Sun beats down with golden rays.
The crops ripen in the sun.
Frightened field mouse begins to run.

Summers hazy Goddess smiles,
At the lazy earthy wiles.

Autumn Fall

Above the moon's Cyclops light,
Under the crisp, leaf-frozen night,
Turning the autumn leaves gold,
Under the foggy frost's hold.
Moving skies, moon on the wane,
Never to pass this way again.

Autumn's face in the shadowed moon,
Undulating wind's whispering croon.
The crunching, crisp leaves fall,
Up against the glistening garden wall.
Moving skies, moon on the wane,
Never to pass this way again.

Fleeting days, fire bright,
All the roofs glistening white.
Love in the cosy autumn wold,
Love the leaves red and gold.

Winter

Winter stretches a skeletal hand,
Cold as ice, frost frozen land,
Stars in heaven, dipping down,
Magic moon wearing winter's frown.

Dredging the snowdrifts,
Ice white freezing fog lifts,
Slipping its snowy curtain,
Life is now uncertain.

In the North Winds blast,
Icicles snap at last,
Sword-like shards of ice,
Fall on hibernating mice.

On the frozen mirror lakes,
Snow hidden, God forsakes,
Its ice cold plummeting depths,
Wailing winter wind's breaths.

Skaters in the coloured light,
Party throughout the night.
Flaming fire, burning bright,
Wonderland, Valentine-white.

Ode to the Moon

Silent song, mirrored moon,
Timely trajectory, Apollo's swoon.
Roaring rockets incline,
Moonbeams light design.

Dream dawn drives,
Astronaut strives,
To reach the hallowed place,
Moon spinning in space.

Celestial sacred light,
Lovers,' long, moonlit night,
Circling the eddy Earth.
Sun central in Galaxy birth.

Mystic mirror reflects,
Deep darkness deflects,
Moonlight strikes the night,
Channel of fantastic flight.

Shadows are the moon's face,
Trees painted with dark lace.
Wolves' moonlight, moaning cry,
Echo in the reflected soulful sky.

Night creatures' awesome glow,
Night fragrances in breezes flow,
Tides pulled by the mirrored moon,
Heady heights, crazy tune.

Sun Dance

Sun dances in the trees,
Blue butterflies in the breeze.
Summer paints the days,
Gold replaces greys,
Day's heavenly rays.
Hot, steamy night,
Colours cluster bright.
In the sunlight bake,
Arid ground forsake.

Sun dances in the glen,
Diamonds dusted again,
On every leafy arbour,
Sails bleached in the harbour.
Summer love meant to be.
Love under the Monkey Puzzle tree,
Summer love meant to be.
Sails bleached in the harbour,
On every leafy arbour,
Diamonds dusted again,
Sun dances in the glen.

Arid ground forsake,
In the sunlight bake.
Colours cluster bright,
Hot, steamy night.
Day's heavenly rays,
Gold replaces greys,
Summer paints the days.
Blue butterflies in the breeze,
Sun dances in the trees.

Dove Stones Reservoir

Rock formations piled above,
Dramatic landscape, perched a dove.
Dove Stones beauty to behold,
Millstone Grit grandeur bold.

The backbone of England defined,
Cascades and reservoir wall combined,
To accentuates nature's cubic design,
Geese and ducks flight line.

The Oyster Catcher swoops,
Grey Wagtails loop the loop.
Great Spotted Woodpecker in a tree,
Elegant Red Kite hovering free.

The mauve moors its secrets keep,
Wild Saddleworth's roaming sheep.
The moor grime rises like its ghosts,
Unto the wildlife that it hosts.

Summer casts her beauty scene,
Stones and rocks dressed in green.
Flowers fragrance the air,
Clouds reflected in water there.

Heather paints the mountain pink,
Spun silk sails rise and sink.
Birdsong nature's music muse,
Wonderful world of birds bemuse.

Morcambe Bay

Lancashire's lush sea swept grass,
Sea pink posies scattered on mass.
Landscape sculptured by the gushing tide,
Groins, bubbling wide waters hide.

Hest Bank teaming with sea life,
Baby Plaice and shell fish rife,
Around Gibraltar's placid pools,
Quick tide encroaches the wise and fools.

Spreading her silver rippling dress,
Golden sunset bathing bless.
Shell ducks with the Cross of Lorraine,
Skim the water's glass pane.

Bore holes gushing sea power surge,
Safe and sinking sands re-emerge,
Bubbling sands, to Barrow the ancient way,
Safe guided walk on a beautiful day.

Race horses prance, a bay and a grey
Love long sunny days on Morcambe Bay.

Rings in the Rain

Rings in the rain, Rainbows remain,
Angels dance.
Lover's trance.
Your hand in mine,
Blessed by the wine.
Rings in the rain, Rainbows remain.
Fragrance in the air,
Blossoms so fair.
Bright stars at night,
Satin so white.
Rings in the rain, Rainbows remain.
Dancing dizzy,
Champagne fizzy,
Skin soft as silk,
Face pale as milk.
Rings in the rain, Blossoms remain,
Casts her bouquet,
Blossoms today,
Beautiful day,
Angels at play.
Rings in the rain, Rainbows remain.
Angels enhance
Lover's trance
Wedding dance,
Real romance.
Rings in the rain, Rainbows remain.

Olympic Games, London 2012

Isles of Wonder, Olympic light,
Olympic Gods, shining bright,
Britain's Olympics in London Town.
Who will wear the Olympic Crown?

Sailing boats from afar,
Guided by a shining star.
Runners, swimmers, athletes and more,
Competing on Britain's shore.

Athens we must praise thy name,
For the historic Olympic game.
Ghosts of Mount Olympus borrow,
Ideals for the Olympic torch to follow.

Competing for Olympic Gold,
New stories will undoubtedly unfold.
God bless those that are competing,
Those whose striving is completing.

Opening ceremony a huge success,
Her Majesty's actions did impress.
The people love the Olympic show,
Olympic Stadium honours bestow.

God bless the stadium of people greeting,
The athletes in their moments fleeting.
The World is watching an Olympic game,
London, Olympics, Medals and flame.

Freedom

Do you think you can die for freedom?
When you die freedom will come?
They'll only shake your empty heart,
And beat it like a drum.

When they give you freedom,
Gasping a gapping last breath,
Followed by the chains that bind,
You can see freedom gagged and blind.

Freedom breathing his last breath.
Can this be freedom's death?
They will tear you up, spit you out,
Dreaming Freedom's shout!

You can fight for freedom,
If only they let you live.
For the words of freedom,
Are all you have to give?

They can tie your hands,
Fill your head with rubber bands,
But you will live for freedom,
For that's all you have to give.

Greece
Inspired by Chrisoula Sirigou.

Sun kissed beaches bake,
Silver waves ripple shake,
Their mantle on the deep blue sea,
Fragrant air, fancy free.

Azure blue sky above,
Greece the country of love,
Dance the heart of music's muse,
Athletic Gods Mount Olympus choose.

Zeus, the King of the Gods on high,
Tossing thunderbolts in his sky.
His symbols the eagle, bull and oak,
Strength and dominance invoke.

His trysts, Gods and Goddess begot,
Athena, Apollo, and Hermes, the world never forgot.
The Acropolis of Athens, the sacred rock stands,
Blue limestone and sandstone feature of the land.

Artesian springs and caves at its feet,
The great city of Athens does complete.
Goddess wonder stretching high,
The Parthenon reaching to the sky.

To Athena Pathados', virgin beauty,
Pays homage, love and duty.
Philides' gold and ivory statue inspires,
Pleasure, love and desires.
The ancient world of ice and fires.

From Sparta's unflinching will,
Modern philosophies spill
Greece the first democracy 508 B. C.
The heart of Europe it has come to be.

No need to believe in what's always there,
Created beauty, land so fair.
Poetry, Homer's Iliad and Odyssey,
Magic muses, music and prophesy.

Under the sinuous Zeus, oak tree,
The Goddess of Love will surely be.

Paris France

Paris is the city of romance,
The Can Can's exotic dance.
France's capital, made for love,
The Eiffel Tower blessing from above.

Nurtured by the great river Seine,
Art and culture's fertile plain.
France gave the Statue of Liberty serene,
Christ the Redeemer, setting Rio's scene.

From Cezanne to Monet,
France always led the way,
From the banks of the Seine,
To the Louvre's world fame.

The Mona Lisa's enigmatic smile,
Designers and couturiers perfect style.
France brought us Haute Cuisine,
Cordon Bleu, as we'd never seen.

For monuments of perfect sculpture,
The world thanks the French culture.

Marbella Spain

She came through the mountain clouds,
That hung over the tops like shrouds.
She looked at the coastline and said, "Mar bella,"
The great Spanish Queen, Isabella.

Mar bella means beautiful sea,
Named by a queen's decree.
The famous Italian explorer,
Christopher Columbus knelt before her.
Sailing from Seville to the Mediterranean Sea,
Beginning his valiant voyage of discovery.
Marbella glistens deep blue,
Rippling with sunlight anew.

Sails like a ghostly cloud,
Dipping herons, heads bowed.
Beyond Africa wearing hazy gown,
To the right, Gibraltar guards with a frown.

From the Blue Mountains she lifts her head,
The beautiful city, on a marble bed,
City of marble, as ever true,
Marbella glistens deep blue.

The Emperor Fountain with its rainbow,
The magnificent sculptures on show.
Salvador Dali, tactile treasures,
Avenida del Mar sculpture pleasures.

Kings, Queens and Sheiks go to shop,
Banus is where the great yachts stop.
Orange Square in the famous Old Town.
City for those who wear a crown.

Spanish Dance

Dance under the star swept night,
Dance in a swirl of colored light,
Dance, hot sand beneath your feet,
Dance with everyone you meet.

It's for the glory of the Lord.
One night forgiveness is abroad.
Dance near the lapping wave.
Dance, the Saint your soul to save.

The bonfires burn bright,
On the beach, through the night,
Barbecues and flowing wine,
Red dresses, senorita's fine,

Elegantly dance to the beat,
Clicking heels in the street,
Twirling, swirling, expressions from the heart,
Flamenco, senors and senoritas dance apart.

They sing a melancholy tune,
To the sea's reflection of the moon.
Guitar music in the breeze,
Under the banana trees.

Fireworks like shooting stars,
Light the midnight sky from afar.
Forgiveness shines from above,
God fills the lonely heart with love.

Passion of Poetry

Rio de Janeiro

Under a smoldering southern sky,
The heart of Rio's Carnival cry,
Samba music in the blood,
Emotional dancing in flood.

Designed for the pure joy of life,
Every expressional excess is rife,
Live life to the drum beat,
Samba schools in the street.

Opulent pageants, dancing night,
Frills and sequins, shining bright,
Bare-foot dancing on the beach,
So many dances to teach.

The life of the city's heart,
Pulsing, throbbing every part,
Live life for the Samba beat,
Samba competitions in the street.

River of January, conquistadors say,
Queen's necklace on a beautiful bay.
Christ the Redeemer blessing from above,
Rio de Janeiro, City of Samba and love.

Saint Patrick's Day

Saint Patrick's shamrock explains,
The Holy Trinity reigns,
The Emerald Isle set in a silver sea,
Emotions, whiskey, Guinness flowing free.

Ireland dances through the dark,
Clash of heels till they spark.
The wearing of the green,
Shamrocks everywhere seen.

St. Patrick came over the sea,
Bringing faith for all to see,
Snakes and sticks,
Miracles not tricks.

All over the world, St Patrick's Day,
Is celebrated, danced away,
Cute colleens, hospitalities flow,
Parades, parties, hearts a glow.

Dancing Dublin dallies,
Racing green rallies,
Life the color of green,
Leprechauns often seen.

Peridot

Winter skies in space and time,
Words and songs no longer rhyme,
Comet lit Hawaiian beach,
Bestrewed sand, sea-swept reach.

Cascade bejewel glow,
Flower's sparkle show,
Fragments of refraction light,
In bright sun and starlit night.

August beauty birthstone,
Deposits, heaven's shimmer shown.
The jeweled comet's pallasites,
Shines at night, moldavite.

Egyptian gem of the sun,
Cleopatra's favorite fun,
Peridot heals the heart,
Aaron's breastplate shines apart.

Twelve sacred stones represent,
Twelve tribes of Israel present.
Green peridot's night time glow,
On Aarons breastplate bestow.

Gold, scarlet, purple and blue,
Linen threads of rainbow hue,
Square peridot topaz green,
Gold tinkling bells heard and seen.

Holiday Romance

Hot the sand beneath our feet,
Under the palm trees, we meet.
Waves lap along the shore.
Who could ever ask for more?

Dreams lost in lover's eyes,
Evoking, deep emotions rise,
Love blossoms near the waves,
The hot, summer sun raves.

We danced to love, without a tune,
Under the bright, moving moon,
Caressing, everlasting romance,
Love's hot and steamy dance.

Dreams are to last forever,
Lover's embrace, ending never,
In this magic summer land,
Memories etched in the sand.

Lovers' dreams are twice blest,
Sometimes they endure with zest,
Shared forever to cherish,
Other times, they just perish.

Beautiful World

Beauty is thy goddess robe,
Saint Elmo's fire, night sky strobe,
The world's mystical globe.

The veils of light illuminate,
The clouds of night vacate,
Love's fire bright consummate.

Blessed the vegetation green,
Life source immortal unseen,
Past world's knowledge glean.

Life energy, eternal day,
Love for all, the eternal way,
Little lamb or bird of prey.

Our World propelled by life force,
On the planet's steady course,
Our natural balance re-enforce.

Earth's gravity is your shoe,
Spinning in the awesome hue,
Rainbows twist in skies blue.
Beautiful world made for you.

Bluebell Days

Bluebells tinkle in the grass,
Winter winds whistling past,
Breathe the fresh spring air,
Hear the season ring fair.

Morning birdsong wakes the day,
Rebirth of the Sun's smouldering ray,
Awakening the barren ground,
With new life all around.

Raging rivers rushing love,
Moving skies screaming above,
Daffodils dance golden yellow,
Coffee coloured clouds clap and bellow.

Little lambs stilted stance,
Skittish foals stiffened prance.
A world of wolds painted green,
Fragrant flowers, spring scene.

Along the River

Lilly pads dark as ink,
In the river slowly sink,
Within its sunset bounds,
Sprouting life abounds.

Shadows shiver, shake,
The oars gently rake,
The weed from bed,
Crocodile's lazy head.

Snaps preoccupied,
Closes lazy eyed.
Sun's red glow, shadows cast,
Lingering light, fading fast.

Moving mound, trickling sound,
Snapping jaws abroad abound.
Gliding the moon-shot water,
Darkness, the Devil's daughter.

Screeching birds, screaming sounds,
The river's depths, death roll drowns.

A Lonely Beach

The silver sea ebbs and flows,
Flotsam and jetsam it bestows,
Distant, darkening sunset glows.

Rolling, rushing spring tide,
Hazy horizon stretching wide.
Dipping birds on the wing,
Soulful sirens sweetly sing.

Life mother earth invests,
Moonbeams magic divests,
Silver rippled richly dressed.

Homeless and devoid of grace,
Running out on the City's race,
Looking for a quiet place,
Life at a slower pace.

Walking along the empty beach,
Life forever out of reach,
Only the seagulls screech.

Time to be touched by dreams,
Life is rarely as it seems,
Catching moonbeams,
In the tidal streams.

A bottle washed on the shore,
With a message in its core,
A secret no one had shared before!

Stale Bread

Wearing your yellow star,
Not tall enough to reach the bar,
A number tattooed on your arm,
Fear prevailed and dead calm.

Your mother, truly brave,
Conspired to save,
Her precious child,
In a world death defiled.

From that evil, starving place,
Hidden and transported, by God's grace.
You came to a foreign land,
No family, no demand.

Stale bread reminds you of your mother.
You never had a brother.
The God of Abraham blessed you,
You flourished and grew.

On the bus to the city,
You saw a flower girl, so pretty.
Jumped off the bus and broke your leg,
She visited you in your hospital bed!

From that day you were caressed,
With love and marriage blessed,
Had fine handsome sons,
A new family had begun.

Yet you could only eat stale bread,
A legacy of the place of the dead.

Holocaust

Eternal light, burning bright,
Sabbath, holy candles light.
Evil came down into the world,
Smoke from the crematorium curled.

Generations were wiped out,
Jewish families, the devout.
Some escaped and bravely fought.
Some refuge and solace sought.

They wore an evil yellow star,
To be easily seen from afar.
The Night of Crystal crashed and cried.
The integrity of a nation died.

Those the Holocaust deny,
God's heaven does decry,
For our eternal God is the same,
The God Abraham, Jesus and Mohammed name.

This evil that was wrought by men,
The righteous remember and condemn.
Those responsible are long dead,
New threats are now said.

The beautiful earth is ours,
To share in God's golden hours.

W. W.2 True Account

A woman and a little girl,
Watched hell's fury unfurl.
Deafening bombardment from the air,
Bringing only death to share.

The buildings burned white hot,
A single sniper takes a shot.
The falling fabrications crash.
Wars devastations fire swept ash

In the rubble of the city,
Mother and child lay, no pity.
She dragged her daughter to her feet,
The destruction was now complete.

Trying to cross a melted tarmac road,
To find a sheltered safe abode,
Cherished child fell head first,
Mother pulled fearing the worst.

The mother tried and tried,
Then mother also died.
A million people fled that day,
Collateral damage, we would say.

How distant from a politician's arm?
Mother and child in death's calm.

Amour
[Inspired by H.H. Princess Maria Amor We Care for Humanity]

Amour, love, the dream of man,
Woman's deep devoted plan.
Amor means no hungry child,
Begging, hair blowing wild.

Searching amongst the rats and mice,
Left-over food, contaminated rice.
Eyes, the saddest soul sight,
Hidden is the child's plight.

Bleeding feet, glass cut bare,
Dirty rags for a child to wear.
Clambering through the bin,
Society's senseless sin.

Amor, love save this child's life,
Poverty is the nefarious knife,
A child of poverty and strife,
Deserves amour, love of life.

Dawn above the Cheshire Plain
Inspired by Dr. Dawn Gibbins and her charity event.

Dawn above the Cheshire plain,
Sunlight's dazzling dance remain,
To touch the globe with love,
Birds circling silently above.

Singing from the ancient woodlands,
Where the loyal oak stands.
Tuned to the ancient vibrant dance,
Lay line lover's circle stance,
Natures prance, treasure trance.

Dreams captured from the sky,
Clouds above the angels cry,
Circling the power of thought,
Ideas love and beauty brought.

Nature wilderness protects.
Jodrell Bank dish collects,
Messages from stars selects.
Bouncing light from the sun,
Beehives cocoons, love and fun.

Nature's beauty set in stone.
Mellow music sets the tone,
Mood magic in the fragrant breeze,
Darkness falls life's at ease.

Passion of Poetry

So Precious Our Love

I searched the earth for you,
Snatched the stars for you,
Flew the ocean for you,
Climbed a mountain for you.

So precious is our love, written in the stars above.

The planets glide together.
Your touch like a feather.
Exploding cascades of light,
Loving you, the starlit night.

So precious is our love, written in the stars above.

Beyond imaginations wheel,
The raw emotions I feel,
Our loves the real deal.
Dreams stretched on angels wings,
Wonderful life our love brings.

So precious is our love, written in the stars above.

Heaven heralded on earth,
Dipping stars, real worth,
Your hand in mine,
A dream so fine.

So precious our love, written in the stars above.

Passion of my heart
No one could tear us apart.

Pre-Historic Storm

Formidable, funnelled hurricane,
Tore the torrid trees, trellis rain,
Whipped the white water again,
Lightening, firing, striking,
Forest floors falling,
Bird's hearts beating,
Moon clouded,
Shrouded,
Red.
The winged monster flew above the trees,
The death cries echoed in the breeze,
Monstrous malignant disease,
Creatures from hell arose,
High the nest of crows,
Skies full of woes,
Monsters swoop,
Hells troop,
Scoop.

Titanic, a Hundred Years

April 1912, Titanic sailed.
The rich of the world hailed,
Titanic the unsinkable,
Lifeboats were unthinkable.

They danced all night, with a shooting star,
Gambling about speeds and sailing far,
On the Atlantic rollers, waves of passion,
Ladies of wealth, breeding and fashion.

It was billed as a historic trip,
Every luxury, Champagne to sip.
Halcyon nights dipped in gold,
Precious memories to be told.

Refraction's mirage floating in the air,
Visionary phenomena, calm and fair.
A million stars bright to see,
Shooting stars, atmospherically.

A huge iceberg loomed,
Ignorant they were doomed,
The Titanic struck its depths,
Cold ice, cold heart, cold deaths.

The icy water flooded in,
Ships pumps couldn't win,
Abandon ship in a lonely sea,
S.O.S radio call came to be.

The poor crawled from below,
The rich told them to go.
Lifeboats only for the few,
Rich women and children, men adieu.

The band echoed across the sea,
The hymn, "Nearer my God to Thee."
The ship in the cold misty ocean,
Disappeared in a downward motion.

Lenses shimmering, air dance,
Temperature bends, trembling trance,
Still atmosphere, stars bright,
Iceberg in the layered light.

Those plucked from a death filled sea,
Only despair could they see.
The faces of their loved ones gone,
Disbelief where joy once shone.

Sixteen hundred souls lost that day,
Sixteen hundred with just time to pray.
A skeleton in a cruel sea,
Absolutely unsinkable, meant to be.

Smokey vapour above Titanic's wreck,
Mushroom cloud the skies bedeck.
Flat, calm, soft, hazy sea,
Horizon blended in entirety.

Lifeboat survivors can only pray,
Titanic's meteorological, mirage day.

Angel Light

Angel golden light descends,
Angel voices earth transcends,
Wafted joy, woven wings,
Son of God, Salvation brings.

Earth exudes escalating joy,
Creation of God's baby boy,
Reflected in Angels' eyes,
Singing spirit through the skies.

Guardians of the holy light,
Guardians of the faith bright,
Angels wrap earth in their wings,
Even the stormy wind sings.

When the Earth is cold with snow,
Beauty blossoms, angel glow,
When darkness seems to smother light,
Angel smiles illuminate the night.

Angels like a distant star,
Watch our world from afar,
Heaven's army, holy host,
Sentinel song, protection post.

Diana, Queen of Hearts

An innocent in a spun silk white dress,
Was given for a royal caress.
She was made of love,
Blessed by God above.

She loved to spend her days,
Helping in many charitable ways.
She visited the homeless, as the sun rose,
No photographers, for whom to pose.

She loved people and was sincere,
But her life was full of fear,
Marriage brought her many a tear.
Still the people came out to cheer.

She was the People's Princess,
She was a beautiful success.
Her orb was the people's span,
They loved her because she was human.

She never knew she was adored,
Now she dwells with the Lord.
Diana, Queen of Hearts in her island grave,
A legend, beautiful, pure and brave.

Prince George, Born to be King

Heaven cries tears of joy,
Thunder, guns, a prince, a boy.
Full moon in the daylight sky,
Illuminations, lightning on high.

Proclamation, the birth of a future king,
Celebration the bells will ring.
Prince Charles's marvellous new grandson,
A new royal life has just begun.

Congratulations played by Buckingham Palace Guard,
Patriotic pageantry, the shining shard,
Westminster Abbeys bells are peeled,
A royal couple's love is sealed.

Tower of London, cannon fire mark,
41 gun salute in London's Green Park.
Into a world of flashing roar,
Camera's all around the door.

A beautiful baby, born to be King,
With love and hope Nations sing,
A precious baby's lovely lullaby,
Sleep pretty baby, please don't cry.

Baptism Day

Blessed by God's Holy Name,
A little baby no sin no blame.
Pouring water a symbol of life force,
To truth and public promises recourse,
Initiation into Christianity,
Soul cleansed original sin free,
Many blessings God's love decree.

Dearest, darling made of love,
Always blessed from above,
Your God, Father, Son and Holy Dove.

Saint Clement Danes, London.

God's island in the strand,
Historic pride of our land,
Oranges and Lemons the bells ring,
The nursery rhyme our children sing.

A thousand years God's holy place,
Knights Templar guard with sword and mace,
Christopher Wren restored thy beauty,
Incendiary ravaged, towering duty.

Perpetual Shrine of Remembrance,
To God eternal reverence,
Angels guard from on high,
Angels flying in the sky.

Allied forces, Freedom Victory Tapestry,
Victoria Cross, forces gallantry,
Sleeps within your hallowed walls,
Prayers, praises, Queen's Standard, history calls.

Memorial to Bomber Command

They stand pillars to the sky,
Phosphor bronze Aces High,
Returned to London Town,
55,000 airman shot down.

Only the shadow shining sun,
Only the shadow sparking gun,
Only the blister blue azure sky,
Where our Hero Eagles fly.

An average age of twenty two,
They were the many and the few.
The Battle of Britain, true blue,
They lived, loyally they flew.

When the engine crackled cry,
Amidst black smoke born to die.
Their protective mantle shaves,
The cloudy cushion, air waves.

Today a Lancaster salutes thy name.
Those airmen who angels became.
Scarlet poppies strafe from above,
Our Queen expresses our country's love.

Now the names wiped from the board,
Engraved and live with the eternal Lord.

Accession Day Diamond Jubilee [6/2/2012]

Accession Day, sixty years,
A beautiful Princess shed tears.
The sad day her father died.
"God save the Queen," the people cried.

Elizabeth became a young Queen,
The face of a nation to be seen,
Promising her life to her country,
Pursuit of steadfastness and duty.

Queen Elizabeth was half a world away,
On her saddest of all day.
From Kenya, where elephants abound,
The Queen returned home to be crowned.

When we go amidst the cheers,
Sixty, loyal, steadfast years,
Spare a thought for our Queen,
The saddest day, she has seen.

The smile on her face is for you,
To cheer the red, white and blue.
Dream walking our Queen re-affirms her vows,
Celebration Gun Salute, a country bows.

The people understand,
Queen's Diamond Jubilee land,

Angel Stone

"Into Thy Hands O Lord I commend my spirit."
[Manchester Cathedral]

The Angel Stone, Saxon throne,
Guards thy southern porch alone.
Worshipper's prayers atone,
Centuries' gargoyle groan.

A thousand years of history stand,
On Manchester's hallowed land,
Great Cathedral to our Godhead,
People's prayers and tears shed.

Doomsday church St. Mary and St. Michael.
Could archangel be the angel's title?
The message in the angel's scroll,
'To God alone we must give our soul.'

Between the Ribble and the Mersey lie,
The holy edifice to God on high.
Dreams caught in thy tower,
Invincible with God's power.

Gothic arches to the sky,
Angels and seraphim's cry,
Shields and flags guard thy beauty,
To God, to country and to duty.

The windows blooded mosaic,
Reflects suffering for history's sake,
The pure white light of grace,
Gives hope to the human race.

The Goddess of the Sand

Praise the Goddess of the Sand,
The girl with the steady hand,
With nimble fingers she picks,
The wires as the clock ticks.

The sun in her care blown hair,
No other Goddess is as fair.
Delicately deft fingers find,
With bravery of heart combined.

Pressure pads all around,
Standing on dangerous ground,
She is our Goddess of the Sand,
A member of an honoured band.

She labours long with every care,
Her knowledge makes her aware,
Booby traps, a second device,
Most pay the ultimate price.

We praise the Goddess of the Sand,
The soldier with a steady hand.

Cry for Freedom

Turrets, the edge of dreams,
Circulating the moonbeams,
Level lush the ground,
Under the years confound.

Striking salute the sky,
Caged birds, eagles cry,
Watching for escape,
Environmental rape.

Pull the clouds beyond the eyes,
Drifting where the eagle cries.
Crested from above,
Freedom, song of love.

Escalator essence chains,
Searing solitary soul remains.

Poppy

Pick your poppy patriotic prize,
Gift of love, soldier souls arise,
Heavenward, died for love,
Died for peace, perfect dove.

Wear your poppy, loving pride,
Each represents a soldier died.
Each gives a gift beyond compare,
A gift in which our people share.

Wounded warriors share your care,
Pride in the poppy that you wear.
Flanders may have become Afghanistan,
Red poppy symbolizing woman or man.

They died in the red poppy fields,
Fell fighting would never yield,
For Queen and country in foreign land,
United Nations, brotherhood band.

Wear your poppy with pride,
Crushed petals, tears cried.
Red poppies falling from above
Representing our Country's love.

Passion of Poetry

1Chrisoula Sirigou and Maureen Brindle Redshift Radio

Mam

Love is the quiet footfall,
The whispering winds call,
The dream dappled summer sky,
The eternal voices crystal cry.

Angels lift thy love,
God takes you above,
The ordinary mortal strife,
To breathe blessed eternal life.

Dance in the starlight shine,
Drink life-eternal's wine,
Joined to the Sacred Heart,
Joined to love ones once apart.

The red, red rose falls for you,
Petal purity, tender true,
Lying on your perfumed bed,
Dew drop tears silently shed.

Kissed to quell her fears,
Bathed her face with tears,
Adieu beloved mother,
Loved like no other.

The Rose

A rose untouched by a thorn,
Dappled dew struck flower forlorn
Holy spring of miracles flow,
Under the stars mystic glow.

Light reflected in satin robe,
Stain glass colored magic strobe.
Veiled by the falling years,
Promises and tender tears.

A white bouquet cast away,
Symbol of a love shared day.
Vortex of passion power,
Beneath the steeple tower.

The rose petals picked,
The photographs depict,
The siren sweetly sings,
Entwined golden rings.

Welcome to this World

All the world is full of love,
Welcome to this world.

Starlight scatters from above,
Precious baby, gift of love,
Welcome to this world.

Sunlight dancing, colored beams,
Day and night pure extremes,
Little sighs, delicate dreams,
Welcome to this world.

Blossom bosom pleasantry,
The gift of life, just for thee,
Expressive beautiful baby.
Welcome to this world.

Memory of white knuckle ride,
Mother and father's pride,
Welcome to this world.

Fingers and toes wriggle free,
New member of the family tree,
Everyone does agree,
You're beautiful to see.

In a tiny babies cry,
The years of history go by.
In the eternal eye,
In the wild winds sigh,
From the mountain high.
Welcome to this world!

Steam Train

Fire-steaming pressure,
Stephenson's careful measure,
Invention's national treasure.

White smoke, sparking trail,
Pulling carriages, sorting mail,
Meeting great ships that sail.

Chugging along the track,
Smoke billowing from the stack,
Pushing carriages back.

Every engine named and numbered,
Great steam power thundered,
Coal wagons, timber lumbered.

Wheel tappers check the train,
Sound for signs of strain,
Sound for flaws yet again.
The Flying Scotsman's singing sound,
Dizzy distance, covered ground,
The most fabulous engine around.

To the world the train became,
A symbol of British fame,
Engineering's ecstatic acclaim.
Crossing all continents,
Travel's torments circumvents,
A rail solution invents.

A train-lift in Petropolis rises,
Electrification, diesel devises,
The Channel Tunnel surprises.
The age of steam began,
A vision of a single man,
The entire world railways span!

City of Manchester

Manchester, my home town,
Wore King Cotton's Crown.
The Manchester Ship Canal, hand dug,
Young Irishmen dying in the mud.

The bridges rise and fall,
To allow the great ships to call.
The Ship Canal flows with mothers tears,
Carrying bales of cotton, for many years.

First from America, in a great ship,
Horses propelled, by the whip.
Still the great mills stand,
Once worked by deft hand.

Where the flying shuttles race,
A great University stands in place.
The Jet Engine, and many more,
Inventions Manchester is famous for.

Emily Pankhurst's house is here,
Votes for women, she felt no fear.
The Bee Gees, Manchester's famous sons,
A long list, I've just begun.

Now the rich apartments overlook,
The Ship Canal roosted by the Rook,
The tall buildings, fight for light,
Hallowed horizon, in the night.

Great City you will always stand,
Manchester, a pinnacle in our land.

Smudge

Smudge came to me one day,
Hungry and in a bad way,
Soon he became top cat around,
White waistcoat and spats abound.

He can jump from tree to tree,
He hides where no bird can see,
His queens are tabbies, three,
Sometimes he hides to be free.

Tabby Longlegs, short haired and tall.
She always has a blustering ball.
She moves at a flying fast pace,
Closes her eyes to make his heart race.

Fluff is a tabby Persian cutey,
Long eyelashes fluffy tale, a beauty,
She rolls on her back in the sun,
Surely she's the only one.

Tabby and white races through,
Is she real, can it be true?
She moves so fast, she's hard to see,
Tabby true love, can it be?

Now they have all moved house,
With white Persian he chases mouse!
A tabby moon near her ear,
A foxy tabby tail, true love, Dear?

Charlie Chuck, Bombing Raid.

Charlie is a Congo Grey,
Parrots like a sunny day,
He always has something to say.

He is never absurd,
Charlie is a clever bird.
Always knows the right word.

His car alarms drive neighbours mad,
Different makes are his fad.
Can mimic every single lad!

Damaged he was rescued,
Prefers chocolate to food,
His language can be very rude.

Damaged tail feathers, relearning to fly,
Charlie could tell you why,
Target the open sky.
Red tail feathers bright,
One day he took flight.
Hadn't mastered landing right.

Through the window he soared,
Caught when the wind roared,
Wobbly, big bird soon floored.
Poor Charlie now was trapped,
Missing posters were dispatched.
A bird nap plan was hatched.

Ransom was duly paid,
Charlie chuck bombing raid!

Passion of Poetry

The Faces of War

War has so many faces,
So many different paces,
Sometimes you think it's not related,
Then you may wish you'd have waited,
To see the results of financial decline,
More powerful than an army's front line.

War has many facet faces,
So many different paces,
The stock markets tumble down,
Politicians playing the clown.
News proclaims the Arab Spring,
Somehow has a hollow ring?

War has so many facet faces,
So many different paces,
Sabotage the credit rating,
Sitting back, just waiting.
War against the mighty dollar, unseen,
Cringing behind a subtle smoke screen.

Van Barfoot Hero [1919-2012]

A giant among men of arms, stands,
From America's southern lands,
Part American Indian, he was proud,
To put the enemy in a shroud.

World War 2 for freedom fought,
His courage was often sought.
Two enemies vanquished, very brave,
Through a minefield, he went to save,
His brothers in arms, from an early grave.

His flame-thrower burned a path,
Destroying an enemy tank with wrath.
Seventeen prisoners, single handed caught,
In Sicily and Anzio he fought.

His Medal of Honor was given in France,
So all his comrades would have a chance,
To share in his glory,
Bravery was his story.

Back at home he fought true too,
To fly the flag, the red white and blue.

Afghanistan War

These are the long days,
When we honor the brave,
Following secret ways,
Always a close shave.

Searching, finding, fighting,
Battling, firing, shooting,
Roadside bombs, a constant danger.
Rest is not to savor.

Dreaming of a peaceful home,
A belligerent war-torn world to roam.
The fight is every waking hour,
Keeping strong is the power.

Undulating under a relentless sky,
With the jet birds screeching cry.

America

America rises like the Rocky Mountains,
Set between two great powerful oceans,
Truth shines like sparkling clear fountains,
Freedom and opportunity aren't just notions.

Encircling the globe with her power,
Smiling on dreams, an outstretched hand,
Pinnacle in many countries needy hour,
Country of wheat bowls, equal poor and grand.

The strength of God shall always be,
With the United States for all to see,
For like-minded people will unite,
To protect our lands, fight for right.

America great land of might,
Leads the world in freedom's fight.

President Obama

See beyond the color cloud,
Hallowed history shouting loud,
The orator of the dappled dream,
Promising the shining sunbeam.

Do they see the weight you lift?
Wielding power in your gift.
Life is in your cherished choice,
Expected a veracious voice.

Responsibility is on your head,
It's not your weight to shed.
History needs an answer,
Stealthily like a panther.

God gave you the mountain to climb,
Mars exploration to define.
A place with the greatest of the great.
To fight for the peoples' financial fate.

Obama Care is more than health,
It's care for people's social wealth.
Care for justice in our wider world,
Care for freedom, the flag unfurled.

Abraham Lincoln

Abraham Lincoln's historic stand,
Immortalized in a canyon grand,
Carved in a mountain's stone,
The Earth's eternal throne.

American, warrior Presidents three,
That fought to keep America free,
Mount Rushmore, Dakota's Black hills,
Guarding with their granite wills.

From a poor Kentucky cabin he came,
Honest Abe, a lawyer became.
He knew about fighting war,
The principles to be fighting for.

Both sides fought for land,
Blooded by righteous demand,
American Civil War, a kind of hell,
Brother against brother, side by side fell.

Northern lady and Southern belle.
Couldn't the traumas of war dispel?
Driven onto opposing sides,
Into opposing armies divides.

Lincoln knew he had to address,
War and slavery with unified success.
States of America's sixteenth President,
Uniting by war and the Fifth Amendment
He is remembered to this day,
Martyrdom, his price to pay,
Now the greatest of the great,
Father of the United States

President John F. Kennedy

The diamond from the Emerald isle,
Prepared to go the extra mile.
Boston's most beloved son,
Fought adversity and won.

Jack Kennedy had the fight.
He stood for what was right.
Hero of the Second World War,
Freedom, he was fighting for.

Commander of a tiny boat.
He sunk the largest ships afloat.
His P.T. Boat was rammed and sinking
Injured he saved his crew from drowning.

From the clutches of a deadly Japanese destroyer,
He led his crew through perilous water,
These were the bravest of the brave,
Jack Kennedy led to fight the wave.

Brave and gravely injured on the shore,
Who could think a man could do more?
Yet he stood for President,
Took the trials God had sent.

Peoples President, in Cold War time,
When warning bells began to chime,
Russia & Cuba threatened nuclear war,
President Kennedy blocked them with more.

President Kennedy saw America strong,
With a United Europe it did belong,
To fight all threats force combined,
He saw the future in his mind.

His target was a man on the moon,
Space travel coming soon,
The innovation it would bring.
Equality was his bubbling spring.

President Kennedy was worshipped worldwide,
His beautiful wife by his side,
Dark Dallas day he cruelly died,
All the free world cried.

Jackie, beautiful and brave,
In blooded suit, unable to save,
Her beloved Presidential man,
Devotedly doing all she can.

She followed the coffin like a Queen,
Little children, bravely seen,
With the burning eternal light,
Shining in freedom's darkest night.

Remember the Souls of 9/11

9/11 infamous date of evil atrocities,
Perpetrated against great American cities,
The world watched as planes went by,
Black clouds billowing from the sky.

As one plane hit disbelief,
Further strikes, anger, grief,
Such evil in the age of flight,
Crystalline blackness, hell darkened night.

Such evil brought such a cloud,
The civilized world in a black shroud,
Demands justice for the innocents that died,
Demands retribution on terrorists worldwide.
Demands solace for those that cried.

Forever three thousand Souls that perished,
In history's eternal waterfall cherished,
For every soul was a tear,
Souls remembered every year.

This was a dastardly declaration of war,
From terror's horrors God protect our shore.

Remember Vietnam

He was just a poor boy,
He didn't have much joy.
Like many thousands more,
The poor boy went to war.

Soldiers were his main stay,
Together they would live and pray,
Upon each other they depend,
To fight together to the end.

They cheered him when he went to war,
They knew what he was fighting for,
Banners flying in the air,
Proving another country's care.

Distant shores of Vietnam,
Hell was the Napalm bomb,
Death from wire trips,
Helicopters were gunships.

Vietcong tunneled down.
How he missed his home town?
Swamps, flies, the battle rages,
At night he turned the Bibles pages.

Wounded, treated with morphine,
Lost a leg, the swamp wasn't clean.
Vietnam wasn't a fashionable war,
Just a wounded soldier, addicted to "draw."

Curiosity Rover

2012 Curiosity Rover landed on Mars.
N.A.S.A.s achievement, reached for the stars.
"Unprecedented feat of technology."
President Obama's glowing oratory.

Promised a man on Mars soon,
An American, like the first man on the Moon.
Three mile high mountains around the landing,
Giant sun on Mar's horizon standing.

Sky crane lowers Curiosity Rover on threads,
Its precious cargo the mother-ship sheds.
Mission control, Pasadena, "Systems Working!"
Mission Mars- geological, biological, standing.

255 million miles to discover,
Supreme technology like no other.
Landing in a pool of Martian dust,
Is the red planet really rust?

Laser zap, liquefied, analyze,
Organic material the mission's prize.
Wheels of technology suspends,
Cameras with fish eyed lens.

Searching for life on Mars,
Cutting edge, no holds barred.
Achievement of the Century created,
The greatest exploration innovated.

The American Princess

The dusky Beauty of the Plains,
Surveys her father's domains,
Standing on a rugged outcrop,
Close to the mountain top.

She wears feathers in her hair,
Leather skirt, her feet are bare.
A shawl of colors keeps her warm,
Outstretching an elegant arm.

She prays to God, the wind whistling,
She prays to the Spirit, snakes hissing,
All the land turns to calm,
Blessed by God's holy balm.

The mystic buffalo wanders free,
As the American Princess we see,
Unplaiting her eagles-wing hair,
Never a maiden was so fair.

She lives in the rivers and the sky.
She lives with the poor where the babies cry.
She lives bringing dream-like hope,
Spirit Princess in the City smoke.

Dark Matter

Dark matter passing through,
Dancing atoms supporting you.
Positron particles unseen collide,
Argon's atom explosion bride.

Flash of luminous light,
Draws distant Galaxies bright,
The secret of universal mass,
The draw of the compass.

Under the snow-capped mountains,
Race to detect fiery fountains.
The Universal eerie evolution,
Of gravitational pull propulsion.

Do you wonder in the night?
What makes the stars shine so bright?
Does dark matter become your light?
Eons evolving stars out of sight.

Perfect Storm

Strength of the perfect storm,
Devastation at dawn,
The seas whipped white,
The black ocean night.

Crushing forces prevail,
In the winds wild wail,
Devastation in its trail,
Water washed city vale.

Boats and houses twisted tossed,
Human lives the heavy cost,
Explosions rent the air,
Darkness licked fire fair.

Nature's forces freed,
Preservations precious creed,
Brave cities luminous lead,
Brave citizens natural need.

Liberty's torch, shimmer shine,
Angry waters, dark decline,
Liberty stands guarding the years,
As a bright age of light appears.

Moon Landing

Engines checked first stage ignition,
Count down, manned moon landing mission.
Apollo 11 engine fired.
Lift off, world inspired.

Apollo rocket risen, first stage ended.
Technology and God their life depended.
Engines jettisoned for weight.
Systems checked all great.

Ignition, the second stage.
The engine burn rage.
Smaller engines travel on,
Soon earth's atmosphere was gone.

Reached speed, on course for the Moon,
More acceleration soon,
Engines jettisoned for weight.
Single small engine firing great.

Lunar orbit coming soon.
Systems go, to land on the moon.
Sea of Tranquility landing mapped.
Eagle Landing-Vehicle checked.

Armstrong, Aldrin, and Collins stand alone,
With the words that set the tone,
The giant step of their bravery,
Achievement of the Land of the Free.

Commander Armstrong kept a safe mission,
Commander from Gemini, iron position,
President Kennedy's star-reaching dream,
Armstrong's giant step caught a moonbeam.

Neil Armstrong first man on the Moon, so brave,
Legend in World history engrave.
The first man to stand on another planet,
Nerves of steel, will of granite.

Presidents see Space exploration,
Bringing glory to the U.S. Nation.
So many spin-off's in our lives,
From the Moon Landing derives.

American flag on the Moon,
Brave astronauts home soon.
Voyage of Discovery without compare,
The mystic Moon that we all share.

Pope Francis

Palm trees bow thy way,
Darling donkey's dearest day,
Sun beating, cloudless sky,
Olives, Christ born to die.

Crossing time, crossing sea,
Franciscan age meant to be.
The humble seagull foretold,
Francis, heaven's keys to hold.

New dawn the apostles stand,
Simplicity guards his hand.
The Holy Hand can write,
Defining the Church's might.

Change comes with every dawn,
Easter Christianity was born,
Francis, faithful Fisher of Men,
Change, gracious God's omen.

People's needs to be addressed,
Love of God and man professed.
Jesuit Father, soldier of Christ prays,
Pope Francis traveling new ways.

Aberfan 1966-2012

The rain pelting on the ground,
A strange eerie moving sound.
The mountain ravaged for coal,
Almost silent the slag heap rolls.

The children sat in the school,
The mountain's revenge so cruel,
All the children of the little village,
Buried in the slag heaps pillage.

115 children of Aberfan,
Parents doing all they can.
It was a most horrific fate,
The school collapsed with the weight.

Miners desperately digging
A village generation dying,
Risen to our heavenly Lord,
Silent sorrow, prayers abroad.

A memorial garden now is blessed,
Where in school, precious souls rest.
A lost generation, forgotten never,
The Lord's heavenly peace deliver.

The coal mine, long shut down,
Slag heaps can no longer drown.
A new school opened in Aberfan today,
Diamond Jubilee Queen, a prayer to say.

Nelson Mandela

Fought for equality, in his rainbow land,
Fought for justice, with the humble and grand,
Fought for the poor and the weak,
Fought for those, who couldn't speak?

From a township so poor,
Often soldiers at the door,
He demanded equality,
He hoped for fraternity.

For the brotherhood of man,
Was his South African plan?
To share the lovely Cape,
Farm the land, tread the grape.

President Mandela lives in history,
He lived in prison to be free,
He abolished apartheid,
Abomination, God decried.

He never wanted to revenge the wrong,
He wanted everyone to belong,
To reconcile all his people,
To look to the church steeple.

Imprisoned for dark, desperate years,
Personal sorrows, family tears,
Until the World's apartheid condemnation,
Made him the Grand Father of the Nation.

Bonfire Night

Tremulously streaming sky,
Firework fiesta firing high,
Stars dimmed with coloured light,
Flickering frantically in the night.

Blasting battle bangs,
Acrid air hangs,
November's churlish chill,
Bonfire on the hill.

Ghosts of gun-powder plot,
Rushing rockets shot,
Guy Fawkes burned at the stake,
Winter's first snow flake.

Potatoes roasting on the fire,
Fireworks flying higher,
Treacle toffees handed round,
Sparklers a swishing sound.

Silver Rains

The shattered stars slow,
Spinning spindle spangled glow,
Heavens herald helium light,
Darkness dipped dappled night.

Hovering halcyon days,
Deep dalliance fading moon rays,
Love's longings cast the spell,
Honeyed hyacinth, bluebell.

Tip toe on the green grassy ground,
Drinking wine, languid lovers abound,
Lying deep in each other's arms,
Drinking loves cherished charms.

Can you catch the streaming light?
The starry glow in the dappled night!
Feel life coursing through your veins?
The misty magic of the silver rains!

Ouija Board

Three young girls sat around,
The Ouija Board they had found.
Anna upturned a crystal glass,
One finger placed en mass.

The glass began to spin,
A finger hit Laura's chin,
The alphabet circled round,
The glass crashed to the ground.

It spelled out, "Go right away.
To the church, respects to pay.
Stand beneath the ancient knight.
Hear the clock strike midnight."

In the churchyard, mist hung low,
Though the trees an eerie glow.
It made the three poor girls shiver,
A dark creature began to slither.

It looked like a massive snake,
The three young girls began to shake,
It rose up from the ground,
An evil apparition to astound.

All the ghosts from the past,
Opened hells chasm vast,
The evil of ten thousand years,
Will crush the mind with its fears.

Clock Tower

Clock is ticking, cobwebs fall.
Rats scurry up the wall,
Beetles burrow down the grid,
A coffin lies with open lid.

In the clock tower corner draped,
In black cloak, bat shaped,
Vampire dripping blood,
Mist for a ghostly hood.
Wakening every night,
From the window taking flight,
Dastardly, dark aberration,
Of evolved, evil creation.

Across the moon diving to earth,
An owl sounding a deadly dearth,
Trill tune of death,
Maiden's breath.

From bat to man the winged cloak,
Natural form, not bespoke,
Vampire, blooded teeth,
Maiden, fragile leaf.

Blown of course in a gale,
In the winds awesome wail,
Vampire struck by light,
Evil creature of the night.
Now vampire crushed to dust,
Clock tower fingers turned to rust,
Maiden floats above the lake,
Spirit, vampire's mistake.

The Cutty Sark

The Cutty Sark's salty beauty seen,
Unveiled by our Diamond Jubilee Queen.
Rabbie Burns' wayward witch,
Wearing a cutty sark to bewitch.

Buxom maid on the prow,
As the waves rise and bow.
Across the oceans with her trade,
Many cargoes, spices pervade.

Three decks, she stands high,
A furrowed cloud against the sky.
Fastest cargo clipper of her time,
Beautiful figurehead so sublime.

Fire couldn't destroy her beauty,
Loyal seasoned ship built for duty.
Bared breasts in a stormy world,
The Cutty Sark with sails unfurled.

Emblem

The Naked Goddess in the sun's shield,
Gunfire strafes the battle field,
So many years the Angels fly,
In shattered sky, battle high.

Safely the Naked Goddess lands,
Protected by God's Holy Hands.
Painted goddess, beauty high,
Protector of land, sea and sky.

The painted lady of the sky,
Tradition as the years goes by.
Angels coming into land,
Following battle command.

Missiles fly to the gushing ground,
Jet powered, the speed of sound
Painted Goddess, beauty high,
Protector of land, sea and sky.

Cat Woman

Cat woman slinks around,
Sliding her high heels across the ground.
Her mink stole hangs from her hips,
She purses her blood red lips.

Her amber eyes shining bright,
Like hypnotic orbs in the night.
She takes anything she needs,
Cat Woman always succeeds.

The police have no leads.
Gold and diamond proceeds.
Invisible in the blink of an eye,
Her song is a bloodcurdling cry.

She calls to her perfect mate.
Tom who will always wait,
To caress her lovely body in a purr,
And stroke her lovely tabby fur.

Cat woman loves the silvery moon,
Alluringly she can often swoon,
Tom does so often croon.
With the dawns dance coming soon,
Only the breeze with its whispering tunes,
Must read the magic in the runes.
Always elegant she is ahead.
No outstretch claw painted red.

House Viewing

The house groans ages past,
Thick walls the years to last,
Peppered with tears and smiles,
The garden has two sundials.

Cold blows with ghosts of death,
Windows frozen ghostly breath,
Neglected for many a musty year,
Children shiver with fancy's fear.

Are the round windows eyes?
Is it true a haunted house cries?
Paint and tender loving care,
Flowers and blossoms to share.

Smell of home baked bread,
Roses blooming brightest red,
The window eyes full of smiles,
Sunshine sparkling on two sundials.

The Loving Cup

Love is yours all the year,
Dreams happiness and good cheer,
I'm just like a loving cup,
The whole world fills me up.

Dance with dazzling days,
Singing perfection's praise,
Dreaming of autumn haze,
Wild woods wandering ways.

The summer sun shines for you,
Shimmering stardust's silver hue,
Over the opulent ocean blue,
The tremulous dreams come true.

Our wondrous worlds conspire,
Filled with passion and with fire,
Love and joy from the heart,
Olive branches worlds apart.

Sergeant Major Jack

"I have come about your Jack,
You must come and take him back.
His waxed moustache, I couldn't resist.
Even though, I was the bottom of his list."

The leggy blonde drew a breath,
Before she began to talk of death.
"He took me for an awesome ride,
Then he lay down and died.

He told of his army days,
Fighting in India's muggy haze.
His father's gold mine in Australia,
His long drawn out legal failure.

A fire raged in the church,
Destroyed the records of his birth.
The brewery helped him out,
But affidavits didn't count.

My husband comes home in an hour,
He thinks that I am his flower.
Please get him out of my bed,
It's no place for him to be dead.

So I have come to you,
Because I don't know what to do!"
"You know he is seventy nine,
Couldn't you find it in your heart to decline?"

Ambulance men said, "No pulse, no breath,
It surely does look like death."
To the hospital they went,
No formalities did they circumvent.

The doctor came out very grave,
"Now my dear you must be brave.
He's asking you to take him home.
It must of course be an alcohol free zone.

Dead drunk is very rare,
He's lucky to have relatives that care.
You can't take him right away
To sober up it'll take a day!"

Solomon Browne Penlee [19/12/1981]

The Solomon Browne fought the stormy sea,
Brave Cornish men from Penlee,
Rescuing sailors from a sinking ship,
Whilst angry waters rise and dip.

The eye of the storm hit the white whipped waves,
Throwing the Union Star against cliffs and caves.
They once were smuggler's haunts,
Now the mighty hurricane taunts.

Lightning struck from the sky,
Illuminating the raging tempest cry.
Wild wind screamed through the ship,
Lifted the hull and begun to rip.

The Solomon Browne went back to save,
More seamen from a watery grave.
A wave picked up the Solomon Browne,
Causing every brave soul to drown.

Thirty years later from Penlee,
Their successors go to sea,
In a little lifeboat to save,
More sailors from a watery grave.

Remember the lifeboat Solomon Browne,
Volunteer crew cruelly drowned,
When the Sea King helicopter failed,
The brave Solomon Browne sailed.

Lilac Days

In the garden wonder born,
Plum trees shade the lawn,
Like parasols filled with life,
Blue tits, robins, blackbirds rife.

The squirrels run up and down,
Cats chase, playing the clown.
The raven decides to swoop,
Pushing the magpie from the loop.

Early rose exude exotic smells,
Under the tree nod the bluebells,
Primroses dot with bright colour,
Snowdrop lights, white with pallor.

Floating from above,
Comes the turtle dove,
Nestling high in the pine,
Whilst we are sipping wine.

Red sky paints the dusky night,
As swoops a hunting kite.
Darkness cloaks until dawn,
Birdsong, harbinger of morn.

The billowing blossom lilac days,
Field mice in bright broom maze.

Tsunami

The Earth rips and rents revenging rage,
Exploding, exuding, moving molten cage,
Deep sea searing quivering quakes,
The surface sea shivers and shakes.

Moving forces fearful mass,
Rise to the surface shattered glass.
Thousands of miles the Tsunami pushes,
Earth's formidable forces rolling rushes.

Devastation for many places,
Death, destruction on many faces.
The power of the rolling wave,
A monstrous wall of water enclave.

Flooding flows demonic demands,
Engulfing, lashing, latent lands,
From its Tsunami sea-bed birth,
Washes salt tears devoid of mirth.

Throw in the Nuclear Power Station,
For lasting complete devastation,
Earth's ecological damnation,
A natural nuclear disastrous creation.

Vesuvius Eruption

Sun peppered burning red.
Ghostly fleeting female fled.
The mountain's sacred dream,
The alchemy of sulphur stream.

The ash from surface dust,
The burning cracking crust,
The storm the harbinger of the flow,
The spitting swirling lava glow.

Molten rocks gushing,
Earths forces crushing,
Hells horrors emerging,
Lava flow smouldering, surging.

Petrified they stand,
Statues bonded to the land,
The world dipped in stone,
Vesuvius' shroud stands alone.

The Unknown Soldier

Shrouded by the veils of loneliness,
Wept for by the silent willows,
Needed by the messenger of righteousness,
Lies a soldier in deaths deep furrows,
Lies courage, bravery, unselfish love,
Lies a rose for patriotism, for peace a dove.
Think not of the silence of the grave,
Forget not the reasons for the death of the brave.
Thoughts of him no memory may recall,
His life as blank as a graveyard wall,
Only a stone with few words inscribed,
Only freedom for which he has died.
This is his legacy to all mankind,
Forget not the gift of peace of mind.

Fallen Heroes

You return our fallen heroes cherished,
In our Country's service you perished.
Forever precious in our home land,
From rocky mounds and burning sand.

Fighting a distant treacherous foe,
Wrapped in a flag of woe,
Through Wooten Bassett or Carterton the coffins go,
Respected by those you'll never know.

The patriotic roses line your way,
The eternal ending of the day.
Old soldiers honour the brave,
The repatriation so grave.

If our tears could bring you back,
A country's prayers could bring you back,
If honor could bring you back,
If love could bring you back?

Our fallen heroes would stand tall,
Heroes in our marble hall.
In the hearts of those who go on,
Brother soldier, family, daughter, son.

We salute you with our silent cry,
From ordinary people to the heroes, that had to die.
Honoring our heroes, who never asked why?
Under Britain's bright sky.

They gave their lives for the all that's right and true,
Home, Queen and Country, red, white and blue.

Sir Winston Churchill

Churchill was a man of his time,
Heart of oak, orator sublime.
The river Thames bore him down,
Past Westminster's parliamentary crown.

A State Funeral was his right.
A gun carriage symbolizing might,
Recognizing his patriotic fight,
To bring the world freedoms light.

Leaves of gratitude entwined with petal of sorrow,
Fall on a grave, in death's long tomorrow.
His words were the waves on which battleships flowed,
His strength led the way on victory's road.

English father, American mother,
His loyalty could be no other,
Land of hope and of the free,
His presence enshrined in history.

His legacy the Second World War won,
England's eloquent international son.
Journalist, soldier, politician, Prime Minister,
He fought against the evil and sinister.

Drink in hand and a big cigar,
A legend in a Rolls Royce car!
The world loved a man art enriched,
His ideas and his words bewitched.

Hell for Men

Moving from the dug-out in the sand,
Crawling with weapons in hand.
Ready for anything ahead,
Blazing sun, burning red.

Now we get up and move,
The dogs in front now approve.
It's safe to advance slowly.
Praying to all that's holy.

Derelict buildings on either side,
Horizons ahead open wide,
No cover beyond, a grave for a bed,
Black smoke where the Taliban had fled.

Roadside bombs a constant fear,
Remembering all we hold dear.
The enemy can just disappear,
Who they are is never clear!

Back-up by fighter jets,
Saviour as the sun sets.
Helicopter swoops like a raven,
Camp Bastion is a haven.

The Falkland's War 1982

Dark destiny jets from Ascension rise,
To regain the Falklands, southern prize.
Vulcan, vibrant vortex swept wings,
Port Stanley's runway destruction brings.

Refuelling amidst the sky,
South Atlantic soulful cry.
Argentina occupying the Falkland Isles,
Combatants brought 7,500 miles.

40 warships taskforce dispatched,
Special Forces on the ground matched.
Penguins in evening dress,
Islanders much distress.

Bomb Alley, San Carlos Bay,
The Royal Navy's sad day,
Exocet missiles target ships,
H.M.S. Antelope sunk, others fire ripped.

Prince Andrew flew his helicopter, so brave,
Our injured servicemen's lives to save.
Waiting our hospital ships,
Cruise liners specially equipped.

Fierce the ferocious fighting fell,
Freezing Mount Tumbledown hell,
245 British servicemen lost,
Was wars horrific cost.
Bravery won the day,
Lives given the price to pay.
The National Arboretum honours the brave,
Souls lost in the Falkland's bitter grave.

Syria

The raped, ravaged cities stand,
Witness to freedom's demand.
The Arab sulphur spring arose,
Terrorist leaders propose.

Skeleton cities show you care,
Dead children you are aware,
The rivers of blood run,
The scenario has just begun.

Divide and conquer is the rule,
Unseeing, unthinking tool,
Power scramble is the race,
Stone is war's unblinking face.

Solomon's wise decision,
Here causes derision,
One side needs to care,
Death in the fire-swept air.

The Arab Spring becomes the Arab Fall,
Extremists ignore Peace's plaintiff call.
Summer's flushing flower is crushed,
Winter's whining, blood blushed.

Today they talk of peace.
Weapons, armaments increase.
People dying on the battle field,
Official stamp, fate is sealed.

Slavery

Walking under a tropical sky,
Talking of love, African day goes by,
Falling in love in the night,
Under the stars of freedom's light.

Grabbed by slavers in the bush,
The forest lost its hallowed hush,
Screams pierce the awe filled air,
Screeching animals frightened there.

Bound and deprived of light,
Taken in the ships deep night,
A world of servitude and pain,
A world without the forest rain.

Evil abounded in the world,
Chained and brutally hurled,
In the seas savage rage,
Slavery sins, evil wage.

Sold no freedom, no love,
A travesty of God above.
International trade, for evil gain,
No tropical sun, no forest rain.

The wind moans a death refrain,
Never to see home again.

Holy Rain

Heaven sends holy rain,
To wash the battle field again,
When the world runs with blood,
Mixing evil with the good.

Who makes the hallowed choice?
Who speaks with God's voice?
Those who fight for peace,
For love and joy to increase.

Heaven sends lightning again,
To clear the unholy terrain.
When the world runs with blood,
Mixing evil with the good.

Where do we find God's holy light,
In the dark, death swept night?
In skeleton cities starvation lingers,
Evil stretches its fiery fingers.

An innocent child finds God's holy reign,
Embattled siege city amidst the pain.

Only a Winters Tale

Orbit ordains your wintry way.
New drab dress every day.
Leaves folded in the ground,
Yuletide blessings abound.

All the days becoming less.

Winter's whining wind transgress,
In her wondrous ice-white dress.
No pity, ponderous she casts her head,
To the skirting, reeling skies of red.
Endless dark drab nubile night,
Reeling winter's flurry fight,
Sleeting veils turn to rain.

Torrents flood the frozen plain,
Along the bursting banks again.
Lighting the world, natures fire,
Enthusing saucy spring to sire.

Presents

Presents, allusion, confusion,
Presents, reality, sonority,
Presents, living, giving,
Present from love evolve.

Resents, lost, cost,
Resents, evolved, involved,
Resents unwilling, filling,
Responding with love revolve.

Events, personal, annual,
Events, anniversary, cursory,
Events Christmas Day, Birthday,
Entirely enticing, living?

Sent, posted, hosted,
Sent, electronically, phonically,
Sent publically, personally,
Single soul mate giving?

Evoke, reflections, perceptions,
Evoke, pleasure, treasure,
Evoke dreams schemes,
Engagement ring shine?

Nocturne, sinner, dinner,
Nocturne, flower, power,
Nocturne, scent, spent,
Nuptials, presents fine?

Thanks, gracious, spacious,
Thanks, quite polite,
Thanks, dear, sincere,
Thoughtful social sign?

Share, living, giving,
Share, recession, expression,
Share, events, presents,
Sharing love divine?

Christmas Night

Homelessness has many faces,
Homelessness has many races,
The teenager from a children's home,
The redundant Hero forced to roam.

Our mean streets frozen with ice,
Foraging in bins with rats and mice.
A cardboard box their only bed,
Fear racing round their head.

A silver icicle hangs like sword,
A child-mother cuts the cord.
Her baby in a sleeping bag,
Abandoned on a cold church flag.

She left her child on stony ground,
The only refuge she had found.
The soldier sleeping on a grave.
Is there anyone left to save?

Under a mirrored moon,
New lovers begin to swoon.
A diamond on her finger bright,
Is this the same Christmas Night?

Christmas Joy

Christmas is a time for joy,
The birth of God's baby boy.
Christmas is a time of cheer,
Celebrating with those most dear.

Valued gifts that are beyond price.
Equal, rich and poor as church mice.
Christmas is the gift of love,
The Holy Spirit, the Peaceful Dove.

A new baby, the life of mankind,
Where future hope, we all find.
Christmas isn't fairy lights, in the sky,
It's the birth of the Christ Child, born to die.

Faith, hope and charity are His gifts,
Our beautiful world, where time heals all rifts

The Ghost of Christmas Past

You hoarded your money away,
Never celebrated Christmas Day.
No feasts with relations or friends,
No presents or hospitality extends.

You were the cold finger that touched the dark,
The dusky cloak against the snow-scape stark.

Under the cloud shivering moon,
Howling silver werewolves croon.
You lay your skeletal bones,
The banging window drones.

You don't care about the starving,
Despise Christmas turkey carving.

Chained to the world, by evil and fear,
Repent and be saved by Christmas cheer!
This very special eve of the year,
Your heart can melt with only a tear.

When at last it's Christmas day,
You can celebrate and pray!

The Spirit of Christmas Present

Today you must change your ways,
Worshipping wealth never pays,
For money is paper after all,
Without faith currencies will fall.

The starving child's swollen belly,
Should turn your heart to jelly.
The soldier who gave his legs.
The street urchin that begs.

Can you save them with a tear?
Can you change the New Year?
Have you got a Christmas dream?
Santa cruising on a sunbeam.

Cold as ice, spin the dice,
Christmas wedding, throw the rice.
Message of enduring love,
Wishing on the stars above.

Christmas Future

In the winter's icy breath,
Christmas future whispers, "Death."
Scrooge must change his way,
Celebrating Christmas Day.

The Spirit rattled a long linked chain,
Scrooge for eternity must maintain.
Of hope and love, he was devoid.
Eternal damnation, he must avoid.

Tiny Tim in his cold grave,
Unless Christmas, Scrooge can save,
Turn Tiny Tim's poverty around,
Before Christmas chimes sound.

The ghost shocked,
The clock stopped,
His nephew shopped,
Tiny Tim hopped.

Scrooge brought turkey for the table,
Presents, money to enable,
Christmas fare, medicine for Tiny Tim,
Scrooge was happy, he'd saved him.

Marley's Ghost was freed from shame,
A shining example, he became.
Scrooge had cast his heavy chain,
Repentance his eternal gain.

Tiny Tim cast his crutch away,
Growing stronger every day.
Scrooge knew cruel consequence,
Came from lack of due diligence.

The vision of the future bright,
Shining in the Christmas night
Singing our carols with love,
The birth of Our Lord above.

Pirate Ship

Floating in a sequined sea,
Mirrored minx flowing free,
Sails of gossamer fulfil,
Ship abandoned at will.

The ghoulish ghost ship sails,
Spectres hold the wooden rails
Through the ocean moon pull,
Deadly forces on the hull.

Raking through the years of plunder,
Oblivious to nature's wonder,
The Skull and Crossbones flag flies.
In the torrid turbulent skies.

Shades of blooded sword conquest,
No chance of eternal rest,
Lookout in the Crow's Nest,
Sun setting in the west.

The pirate ship must sail,
Locked in the tempest flail,
In the storm and hail,
Lost in time, the spirits wail.

The years through a veiled mist,
Sapphire sea sun-kissed,
A dogged drone takes them out,
No time to turn about.

Passion Flower

Excited bodies touch,
Accidentally crocus crushed,
Spring's sparkle in the air,
Spring blossom's draping there.

On spring's high tide,
Catch a magic mystic ride,
Budding bluebells bloom,
Bursting Spring Rivers loom.

Spring storms light the sky,
Spring lambs bleating cry.
New life the earth confounds,
New grass and flowers abounds.

The stately stags lock horns,
As the new day dawns,
Red slashes the spring sky,
Eagles swoop from on high.

Touched by loving hands,
The wild wide world expands.
New lovers light the night,
Passion flower burning bright.

The Spirit of Love

You are my love passion sent,
Your former lovers you repent.
The silky softness of my desire,
The dreams of love that do conspire.

To touch you is my ecstasy,
Heaven's horses riding free.
My mind in a dizzy daze.
My body goes its own ways.

In the earthy passion faze,
In hot and steamy summer days,
When I can catch my breath,
Without your love would be my death.

The golden garlands that you throw,
The lingering love that you bestow,
You hear my whispering in the breeze,
Your loving ghost, be at ease.

Over the lake my spectres rise,
Only to look into your eyes.
When I twist, in the mist,
Remember it was you I kissed!

The Ghostly Coal Miner

Deep down, dark night, coal bright,
Flickering, a solitary miner's light.

The ghostly miner works the face,
Below the screeching spinning wheel race,
That raised the creaking lift,
In the valley's sinking rift.

His ghostly hammer knocks,
Against the fallen rocks.

Black coal dust in the air,
Water waist-deep there.
The gaseous cloud ignites,
Exploding deadly light.

A hundred years the minor toils.
A hundred years the cable coils.

His ghostly hammer knocks,
Against the fallen rocks.
No escape from the deep,
No rest, no eternal sleep.

Love and War

The swirling dance of life's fire,
Entraps our souls in deep desire,
And as the song of nature cries,
From the starlit moon shone skies.

He stands amidst the ruined streets.
Only his automatic fire repeats.
They say everyone is born to die,
A hand held rocket is his reply.

What ghosts will rise from this place?
What deathly apparition with a human face?
Life is burned into the sand,
Death, untouched by human hand.

The blooded moons sanguine light,
Sheds solitude silent soul sight.
The lover-soldier sings his song,
Glory amidst Angels' throng.

Night Witch

Sunburst red, twisting trails,
Flowers dance, the sun-drenched sails,
Hemline tips tantalizing,
Salsa skips sensitizing.

Music muse deftly dreaming,
Beat becomes sensuously steaming,
Life's lusty exotic exposure,
Crimson cradles golden composure.

Sultry dancing, silent sky,
Red reflections burning eye,
Stoically setting in the west,
Bleary blanket night quest.

Stars hang in nature's dizzy dome,
Lighting lovers hurrying home,
Moonlight moves the Night Witch,
Showers silver shadows to bewitch.

Summer scents pervade the air,
Balmy beauty fancy fair.
Night Witch crimson fire spell,
Emotion's desire to compel.

Honey

Honey in the tree,
Pollen gathered by the bee,
To energize me.

Honey coloured hair,
My honey has skin so fair,
A black belt beware!

Rich honey lit sky,
The sunset colours on high,
The dark clouds float by.

Honey is my love,
We are like two turtle doves,
In the sky above.

Honey is my sweet,
Each day busy bees compete,
To make life complete.

Dreams

Dreams are the feathery wisps of night,
The silver slithers of moonlight.
The weary night wind cries.
The spinning silent world sighs.

For all the lost dreams of man,
Tumultuously twisted earthly span,
Where the nightmare tempest arose,
Squirming in a nest of crows.

Some dreams from the heart arise,
From lovers of the good and wise,
With angel voices rise above,
Flying, fluttering like a turtle dove.

Twisting in the day-dream lit light,
Avoiding the wars and man's might,
Fighting for the cause of holy right,
Through the worlds darkest night.

Peace and love are dreams to stay,
The harbinger of New Year's Day.

St. Joan of Arc [1412-1431]

Saint Joan of Arc stood strong.
Fought for France against wrong,
Died a heroine burned at the stake.
She gave her life for country's sake.

Great French heroine she became,
The lovely maiden of Loraine,
A humble girl, risen high,
Burned against a fire raged sky.

Nineteen years she lived on earth,
Heart of love, patriotism and worth,
God sent her a vision from above,
To fight for freedom, for France's love.

Unflinchingly into Orleans charging,
Leading, winning, the battle raging.
It was the Hundred Years War,
Others had tried to win before.

Charles the Seventh, crowned King of France,
St Joan of Arc watched, in a holy trance.
Maid of Orleans in a barbaric time,
Her killing, a horrendous crime.

Condemned for heresy,
Her trial was a fallacy.
Heavenly vision's hallowed light,
Arch-angels and Saints shinning bright.

The executing British soldiers cried,
As the Maid, so young and lovely died.
They scooped her ashes, loving pain,
To unite her with France once again,

They scattered her ashes in the Seine,
Holy Martyr, Maid of Lorraine.

MISSY CAT'S CHRISTMAS FAIRY

Maureen Brindle Author   Patricia Eichler Illustrator

Thank you

I hope you enjoyed Beloved Isles. Poetry makes a great gift! Patricia is reading and signing our children's book in Ohio.

Missy Cat's Christmas Fairy.
Children's poetry picture story
Available worldwide now.

More information on my website.
Best wishes, Maureen Brindle

www.maureenbrindlepoetry.com

Printed in Great Britain
by Amazon.co.uk, Ltd.,
Marston Gate.